To

Diving Into™
Wine

Your Springboard to Wine Discovery

Diving Into™
Wine

Your Springboard to Wine Discovery

By Wayne Belding
Master Sommelier

Vintage Advantage Press
Boulder, CO

Diving Into Wine: Your Springboard to Wine Discovery

Published by Vintage Advantage Press, 1410 Ithaca Drive,
Boulder, CO 80305, vintageadvantagepress.com

Author	Wayne Belding
Project Manager	Richard Peck
Editor	Susan B. Peck
Book Design	Nancy Cutler, Midnight Oil Design, LLC

ISBN: 978-0-615-33199-7

10 9 8 7 6 5 4 3 2 1

To Miriam and Scott

Contents

∿

ACKNOWLEDGMENTS

Although my thought process for this book started decades ago, the reality of publication would not have been possible without the efforts of a few key people. Thanks to Richard and Susan Peck for their sage advice and editing throughout the process of moving from loosely formed ideas into the printed form. Nancy Cutler of Midnight Oil Design kept the project in focus and moving forward at every juncture.

Throughout my years in the wine business, I have been treated with wonderful hospitality and generosity by grape growers and winemakers in many countries. They are truly on the front lines of the intricate transformation of grapes into wine and their knowledge and experience is the foundation of my own. This book could not have been written without their answers to my many questions.

I thank my fellow Master Sommeliers, both in the U.S. and abroad, who have provided an inspiring community of wine professionals that has regularly energized and revitalized my passion for wine, and for sharing this passion with others. I have drawn tremendous insight from their diverse experiences.

I offer special thanks to Sally Mohr, my fellow Master Sommelier and business partner in Boulder, Colorado, for more than two decades. We have spent those years demystifying wine and opening new vinous frontiers for our many customers. We have been privileged to discover and share thousands of wines over that time. Her brilliant sense of wine and its elemental pleasures is echoed throughout these pages.

Wine & You

 Wine is a fascinating subject, but it can be a frustrating one as well. The range of easily available wines provides an incredible and enticing variety of aromas and flavors. This sensory allure virtually compels winelovers to learn all they can about the reasons for a wine's stellar characteristics.

Too often, though, those with a kindling interest in wine find themselves awash in a bewildering barrage of facts about vintages, producers, grape types, wine laws, and who knows what other vinous trivia. Plus, there is truth in the stereotype of the haughty wine snob (your know-it-all neighbor or co-worker, perhaps), ready to scorn your wine choices with a dismissive wave of the hand.

Given those social and information barriers, it is not surprising that the potentially interested wine consumer frequently turns to the relative safety of a well-known brand name and thereby never experiences the sensory delights that are literally within reach. How can an interested consumer learn more about wine without devoting inordinate amounts of time to the subject?

It is common wine wisdom that *you* are the ultimate arbiter of what constitutes good wine for you. There is truth in that axiom and in the final measure, it is indeed true—you know what you like and you should buy for your own taste.

All of us know, however, that our tastes can change with experience. It's likely that very few espresso aficionados enjoyed their first cup of coffee, but they grew to appreciate the rich and bracing bitterness of a skillfully brewed cup. It is not unusual for those who are starting their wine exploration to be drawn to sweeter styles. After all, we are a nation that has grown up on sweet and/or fizzy beverages.

As our experience grows, though, most wine enthusiasts find that their preferences expand. While we may not like every wine we taste, we can recognize absolute quality. If you never experienced seafood fresh from the sea or a perfectly ripe wild strawberry, it's hard to state that you don't like them. So, try as many wines as you can, and you will define your preferences so you can concentrate on an elaborate exploration of your favorites.

Let's steer through the adjectives and get to the heart of the subject—wine is a beverage fermented from grapes that is meant to be drunk with friends, family, and food. It smells good, tastes good, and can enhance nearly any meal.

Usually people remember that a wine was good, but are unable to articulate exactly why. The interest is kindled and the question of why this wine, among all the wines available, was so delightful. Was it that this particular wine had an especially attractive aroma? or was it the flavor? or the finish? It is difficult to translate sensory experience into words, but it is necessary to do so if you want to recall characteristics of favored wines. To help remember specific wines, we will explore ways to assign words to the range of aromas and flavors found in wine.

If your interest is piqued, you will want to learn a bit of the story behind a wine you like. If you explore just one new wine a month, you will have a dozen in your repertoire by year's end—plenty of information to successfully navigate through a wine list.

Where Wine Is Made

Wine is made throughout the world, mostly in a band of 30° to 50° latitude in the northern and southern hemispheres. At latitudes higher than that mark, it is difficult for grapes to ripen. At lower latitudes, grapes can grow, but the heat and often-tropical climates make fungal and insect-borne diseases a problem and the hot climate generally results in dull wines with little character.

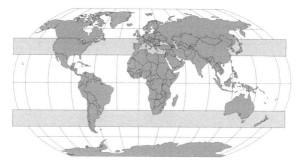

Wine is typically described as Old World or New World, based on its origin and the traditional styles of wine making in the region. Europe is considered Old World, while the United States, Australia, South America, and South Africa are the primary New World regions.

While the most famous Old World wines are from France, Germany, Italy, Portugal, and Spain, a great deal of wine is made in Austria, Hungary, Greece, Switzerland, and throughout Eastern Europe.

We start with a more detailed look at France and Italy, because French wines are the standards by which others are measured and French wine styles have been emulated by winemakers throughout the world. Italian wines, while lagging behind the French in wine snob prestige, provide a range of style and character that is unparalleled.

France

The map shows the most famous of the French wine regions:

BORDEAUX: Located near the Atlantic Coast of southwest France, the Bordeaux region grows Cabernet Sauvignon, Cabernet Franc, and Merlot as the primary red grapes; Sauvignon Blanc and Sémillon for whites. The maritime climate has profound impact on the growing conditions here.

BURGUNDY: Located in east-central France, Burgundy is known for Chardonnay (white) and Pinot Noir (red). Adherents argue that these are the finest expressions of these two grapes in the entire world.

BEAUJOLAIS: Although often considered as part of Burgundy, the Beaujolais region is known for the Gamay grape grown in the granitic soils of the Beaujolais Mountains, which yields a distinctive, grapey, and fresh style of wine.

ALSACE: In far northeastern France, Alsace lies in the rain shadow of the Vosges Mountains and is the driest and sunniest French growing area. It is most noted for dry white wines from Riesling, Gewurztraminer, Pinot Gris, and Pinot Blanc grapes.

LOIRE VALLEY: France's longest river, the Loire, flows 600+ miles from the center of France to the Atlantic. Chenin Blanc, Sauvignon Blanc, and Muscadet are the primary white grapes. Cabernet Franc is used for the best-known reds.

RHÔNE VALLEY: The Rhône flows into France from Lake Geneva in Switzerland and then south to the Mediterranean. The region is best known in its northern reaches for red wines of the Syrah grape (Hermitage, Côte Rôtie) and Grenache-based blends in the south(Châteauneuf-du-Pape).

CHAMPAGNE: The chalky soils of Champagne in northern France yield the most complex of the world's sparkling wines. Chardonnay, Pinot Noir, and Pinot Meunier are the grapes here.

Italy

Italy encompasses a vast range of growing areas, wine styles, and grapes that are becoming more widely sold and recognized. Although all 20 regions of Italy produce wine, these are the most often seen areas:

PIEDMONT: Located in the foothills of the Alps in northwestern Italy, Piedmont is the source for red wines of the Nebbiolo grape (Barolo, Barbaresco, etc.), as well as Dolcetto, Barbera, and more. White wines from Moscato, Arneis, Cortese, and other grapes are produced here as well.

VENETO: The region encompasses the city of Venice and much more. White wines from Garganega and Trebbiano grapes (Soave) and reds from Corvina blends (Valpolicella, Bardolino, Amarone) are widely seen.

TUSCANY: Here, in the rugged central hills all the way to the coast, the Sangiovese grape under several names produces the red wines of Chianti, Brunello di Montalcino, and more.

APULIA: The "heel" of Italy's "boot" is a relatively flat and very productive region with widespread plantings of Negroamaro and Primitivo (cousin to California's Zinfandel) that yield heady, robust reds.

SICILY: The island at Italy's "toe," offers a remarkable range of wines from coastal and montane vineyards. Reds from the native Nero d'Avola and Nerello Mascalese can be impressive. Whites from Inzolia, Grillo, and Catarratto grapes are full-flavored and dry.

There is much to discover beyond these most widely seen regions. Friuli in the far northeast of Italy yields very high quality white wines from Pinot Grigio, Chardonnay, Sauvignon Blanc, and a range of native varieties like Friulano, Ribolla Gialla, and Verduzzo.

The Marches, on the east coast opposite Tuscany, offers crisp whites from the Verdicchio grape and reds from Sangiovese and Montepulciano.

The Campania region encompasses the city of Naples and is a source of exotic white wines from the Falanghina, Greco, and Fiano varieties plus robust reds from the Aglianico grape. Many other native varieties are used in southern Italy and this area is a wonderful source for new discoveries.

Spain

Spanish wines cover a wide spectrum of styles. Moving from west to east across northern Spain we find the crisp and fragrant whites from the Albariño grape from Rías Baixas, exciting reds from the Mencía grape in Bierzo, traditional styles and more from Tempranillo grapes in Rioja and Navarra, the powerful reds from Priorat and environs, plus the sparkling wines from Catalonia.

Central Spain offers aromatic whites from the Verdejo grape in Rueda, powerful Tempranillo-based reds in Ribera del Duero, luscious and elegant wines from Garnacha grapes in Cariñena and Calatayud, and heady reds from Bobal and Monastrell grapes from Jumilla and Alicante on the Mediterranean Coast.

Southern Spain offers the fortified wines of Sherry, Montilla, and Málaga.

Germany

Riesling is the great grape of Germany with superb and distinctive examples ranging from bone dry to luscious and sweet styles. The Mosel Valley offers delicate wines with their subtle sweetness perfectly balanced by racy acidity. The Nahe, Rheingau, and the Pfalz provide many richly-textured, dry Rieslings along with the traditional sweeter styles.

The Silvaner grape makes world-class wines in Franconia and excellent Pinot Noirs (here called Spätburgunder) are found from warmer sites in the Ahr Valley, the Rheingau and Baden.

Germany is also a source of many grapevines
created by crossings in nurseries with a goal of breeding
earlier ripening varieties. Many are absorbed into generic
blends, but consumers can occasionally find a Scheurebe,
Kerner, Huxelrebe, or other unusual variety bottled separately.

Portugal

The Atlantic influence shows in the fresh and fizzy crispness
of Vinho Verde in the north. The hot upper reaches of
the Douro Valley are home to Port production and the
Touriga Nacional grape, among others. Areas like Dão,
Tejo, and Alentejano are best known for spicy reds from
native grapes.

The Peninsula de Setúbal, south of Lisbon, yields fine
aromatic wines from Muscat grapes in styles from bracingly
dry to headily sweet.

The volcanic island of Madeira makes famous, fantastically
ageable, fortified wines from Sercial, Verdelho, Bual, and
Malmsey grapes.

Greece

There is much more to Greek wine than Retsina, the pine
resin flavored wine so ubiquitous in Greek restaurants.
World class whites are made from the native Assyrtiko
grape on the island of Santorini. The Peloponnese yields
fragrant and floral whites from the Moschofilero and
luscious, juicy reds from the Agiorgitiko grape.

The northern area of Macedonia offers exotic and nuanced
reds from the Xynomavro, plus floral whites from the Mala-
gousia. There is much to discover in Greece.

Austria

Grüner Veltliner is the benchmark Austrian grape, widely
grown on the often-terraced banks of the Danube River,
upstream from Vienna. Fine Rieslings are grown here as
well. Austria is justly noted for the dessert wines from
Burgenland on the Hungarian border, and for intense dry
whites from Styria in the south of the nation.

The Rest of Europe

More and more wines from other European nations are
finding their way to the international market. Hungary
offers the legendary dessert wines of Tokaji, plus much
more. Switzerland yields a range of crisp whites and light
reds. The Czech Republic, Slovakia, Slovenia, Croatia,
Bulgaria and Romania all have long winegrowing traditions
and will offer their wines more widely in decades to come.

United States

The New World tradition often eschews the Old World
predilection for blending and instead emphasizes the grape
variety on the label. American consumers are very familiar
with California wines, with the Napa Valley as the iconic
hub of the industry. California is a large state and there is
much to discover from Sonoma, Mendocino, Monterey, and
Santa Barbara and beyond.

Pinot Noirs from Oregon have gained international acclaim
and Washington State has a rapidly growing wine industry.
There are burgeoning wine industries throughout the rest of
the US (and their neighbor to the north, Canada) and excellent wines are made in many of them.

Australia

Also in the New World, Australia offers much more than the famous brands. Chardonnay is successfully grown throughout the country and often blended across regions under the Southeastern Australia designation. Superb wines are made in New South Wales, most notably in the Hunter Valley, north of Sydney, where Shiraz and Semillon grapes are widely seen. Victoria is home to the city of Melbourne as well as a wide range of wine styles. The Yarra Valley is noted for Pinot Noir and Chardonnay wines. The inland areas of Heathcote, Bendigo, and Nagambie Lakes yield powerful Shiraz and Cabernet Sauvignon wines.

South Australia produces over half the nation's wines and offers superb reds and whites from many locations. Luscious and velvety Shiraz wines from the Barossa Valley are famous. Pure, ageable, dry Rieslings come from the Clare and Eden Valleys. The McLaren Vale has many old vine Grenache vineyards. The Adelaide Hills Pinot Noirs are gaining worldwide recognition and refined Cabernet Sauvignons from Coonawarra have long been famous.

Western Australia has many fine Cabernet Sauvignon and Merlot bottlings from the Margaret River region as well as enchanting, perfumed whites from the Verdelho grape variety.

New Zealand

The North and South Islands of New Zealand offer a range of fine wines. North Island areas like Hawke's Bay are warm enough to ripen Cabernet Sauvignon.

Marlborough, on the South Island, is justifiably famous for its assertive Sauvignon Blanc wines. Central Otago on the South Island is gaining international acclaim for its Pinot Noir wines.

Chile

A span of winegrowing valleys transects the central part
of this long nation on South America's west coast.
Cabernet Sauvignon, Merlot, and Carmenère thrive in the
Aconcagua, Maipo, Colchagua, Rapel, and Curicó Valleys.

Sauvignon Blanc and Chardonnay do well in the Casablanca
Valley. Pinot Noir shows promise in the coastal areas of
Leyda and San Antonio.

Argentina

Argentina is one of the world's largest wine producers.
Malbec from Mendoza is well regarded throughout the
wine industry, but Cabernet Sauvignon, Merlot, Syrah, and
Bonarda all make quality reds here.

White wines from the Torrontés grape are sourced from the
high altitude vineyards of Salta in the north.

South Africa

South Africa has perhaps the most dramatic scenery in
the wine world, with vineyards nestled below soaring cliffs
of the many mountain ranges. Chenin Blanc (sometimes
called Steen), Sauvignon Blanc, Sémillon, and Chardonnay
all do well here for whites.

Syrah/Shiraz, Cabernet Sauvignon, Merlot, and Pinotage,
the South African cross of Pinot Noir and Cinsault, are all
widely planted.

How to Taste Wine

 You have been training your senses since you were born. Think of wine as just another food. What types of foods are your favorites? Do you revel in hot, spicy flavors or do you avoid the heat? Your mood can even change what you prefer to eat and the same goes for your beverage. If you are looking for comfort food, what type of wine is going to help with that calming effect? All of these elements should be taken into account when you taste a wine. Now, let's get on to the actual tasting process.

Steps To Tasting

We use the senses of sight, smell, and taste when evaluating wines. Most often, you would rather just enjoy a glass and not think about it. Wait until you're in a studious frame of mind before you sit down to analyze the elements of fine wine. Better yet, pick two different wines so you can compare as you go. Here's how we approach wine evaluation:

SIGHT: The visual impressions are the most straightforward. Look at the color and clarity of a wine. Observe its intensity as well as its hue. Note how the color changes from the middle of the glass to the rim.

White wines often begin with a pale color accentuated by hints of green. As they age, their color becomes deeper, more yellow-gold, and may ultimately grade to amber.

Red wines range from nearly opaque and blackish in color to a very light ruby, and every shade in between. Reds often begin with a vivid, purplish hue which matures into crimson and ruby colors and ultimately develops into brown, mahogany, and orange hints. The color of a wine gives clues as to its origin, grape variety, vinification, and age.

Much is made of the "legs" of a wine—the tears that form on the side of a wine glass after swirling. The presence of the tearing effect is a physical phenomenon. Wine is alcohol and water in solution and alcohol has a lower surface tension and temperature of evaporation than water. The interaction of water and alcohol involves the capillary action of the fluid and the respective differentials between the surface tension and evaporation points of the two fluids. The reasons are complex, but (Newtonian physics aside) the result is that the tearing effect is more pronounced in higher alcohol wines. The phenomenon is accentuated even more when you add additional substances like sugar and glycerol to the mix.

The myth that more obvious legs are the sign of a better wine comes from the history of northern growing regions where the climate only permits full ripening four years out of ten. In these areas, the fully ripe years yielded better wines, and wines with higher alcohol and more pronounced legs.

SMELL: Assessing the aromas of a wine is perhaps the most difficult part of wine appreciation. Many wines have distinctive scents, which have different meanings to individual tasters. One of the best ways to differentiate between wines is to consider the aromas in terms of other fruits.

White wines can bring to mind scents of apples, pears, peaches, pineapples, melons, citrus fruits, and figs, among others. Think about whether the aromas recall fresh fruits, cooked fruits, or dried fruits.

Red wines can be reminiscent of red fruits—strawberries, redcurrants, raspberries, red cherries—or black fruits—blackberries, blackcurrants, plums, black cherries—or both. The same fresh/cooked/dried fruit analysis applies here as well.

In addition to fruit aromas, wines often exhibit scents that result from the site in which the grapes were grown, specific grape varieties, vinification methods, and length of aging.

Oak barrels can impart a distinct caramel, vanilla-like, or baking spice (cinnamon, clove, nutmeg, etc.) component to both red and white wines.

Look also for floral, spice, and herbal smells. Once noted, these elements can give you a mental, sensory benchmark by which you can evaluate future tastings. Scents similar to roses, honeysuckle, lavender, violets, bay leaf, tobacco, allspice, anise, and black pepper are all found in wines. Older wines are likely to exhibit aromas reminiscent of earth, mushrooms, truffles, tar, and coffee bean.

You may find it useful to write down your impressions of a wine's olfactory profile. Doing so helps you mentally catalogue a specific characteristic and makes it easier to identify the same characteristic when you experience it again.

TASTE: The flavors of wine are usually a confirmation of the sensory elements detected in the aromas. The human olfactory sense is far more discerning than the sense of taste. On the palate, you find the same range of fruit flavor similarities, as well as the herbal, spice, and earthy elements that are evident at the nose.

You may find it helpful to break down the flavor of a wine into three parts: the first impression, the middle, and the finish.

Some wines have an initial burst of flavor that is not backed up by any richness or concentration. That's the definition of a simple wine. "Simple" doesn't mean it's not enjoyable. In fact, a simple wine may be exactly what you crave at the moment.

Other wines can impress with layers of fruit, spice, and other nuances. These flavors can cover the middle of your tongue with diverse sensations. Tasting such a wine is as if all your flavor receptors are activated. If there are lots of flavors—fruit, floral, herb, and spice—that's what we wine geeks mean when we talk about "complex" wines.

The texture of a wine is important, as well. Think of the mouthfeel of skim milk compared to 2% milk, whole milk, half & half, or heavy cream. You can assess wine textures in the same manner. Some will be light and evanescent, others will be rich and palate-coating.

There are physical characteristics of wines that are very important elements in the impression they make. Acidity is present in every wine. Acidity is the tart component that activates your salivary glands and makes your mouth water. Wine is a very acidic beverage compared to other fluids we drink, but wine can vary from tart, crisp and mouthwatering to soft and creamy-textured.

Residual sugar leaves a sweet impression on the tip of your tongue. It is often mistaken for other elements in a wine. Ripe fruit characteristics have a sweet impression on the palate as do alcohol and oak. It takes a little work to isolate and recognize the impact of sugar. You can experiment by making your own sugar solution and adding it in small quantities to a dry wine and see how it changes the impression.

Tannins are present in red wines. Tannins are the mouth-drying sensation that lingers on the palate. Tannins are extracted primarily from the skins of the grapes, along with color. Tannins can also be leached from oak barrels. Tannins are natural antioxidants that allow wines to age. They can range from barely perceptible to fierce and dominant, depending on the grape variety, the age of the wine, and the vinification techniques.

Alcohol is another key ingredient for all wines. Most often, alcohol is sensed as warmth at the back of the throat after you taste a wine. Although alcohol is an essential element that provides body and texture in wine (try a de-alcoholized wine to see what we mean), wines with too much alcohol can seem like an inferno after a few sips.

The length of time a wine lingers on the palate should be noted. This characteristic is the finish. The winetaster uses the terms "long" or "short." Also note whether the finish is intriguing or pleasurable. An excellent wine should entice the consumer to take another sip. If it doesn't, try to discern what characteristic is not pleasing.

These thoughts are just an overview of some of the parameters you can apply to winetasting.

Even if you get involved in a more structured tasting process, please don't forget to enjoy the wine you are tasting. After all, that's why people become interested in wine in the first place. Intense study can enhance your appreciation of a wine's salient characteristics, but only if you let yourself appreciate the wine as a whole and not just as an assemblage of components.

Enjoy your tasting. The real pleasure is in drinking the wine, not the analysis.

Describing Wine

As you use sight, smell, and taste to learn more about different wines, you need terms to help you describe what your senses are recognizing.

FRUITS FOR WHITE WINES:

- ○ Lemon
- ○ Lime
- ○ White Grapefruit
- ○ Pink Grapefruit
- ○ Orange
- ○ Tangerine
- ○ Green Apple
- ○ Red Apple
- ○ Yellow Apple
- ○ Pear
- ○ Peach
- ○ Apricot
- ○ Green Melon
- ○ Orange Melon
- ○ Pineapple
- ○ Mango
- ○ Guava
- ○ Papaya
- ○ Lychee
- ○ Fig

FRUITS FOR RED WINES:

- ○ Raspberry
- ○ Strawberry
- ○ Red Cherry
- ○ Redcurrant
- ○ Cranberry
- ○ Red Plum
- ○ Blackberry
- ○ Black Cherry
- ○ Blackcurrant
- ○ Blueberry
- ○ Black Plum
- ○ Prune
- ○ Raisin

FLORAL:

- ○ Orange Blossom
- ○ Honeysuckle
- ○ Violet
- ○ Rose
- ○ Lily
- ○ Lilac
- ○ Gardenia
- ○ Lime Leaf

HERB/VEGETAL/EARTH:

- ○ Rosemary
- ○ Thyme
- ○ Cut Grass
- ○ Asparagus
- ○ Lavender
- ○ Marjoram
- ○ Bay Leaf
- ○ Sage
- ○ Mint
- ○ Dried Leaves
- ○ Eucalyptus
- ○ Anise
- ○ Tobacco
- ○ Sandalwood
- ○ Pine
- ○ Green Bean
- ○ Jalapeño Pepper
- ○ Green Bell Pepper
- ○ Chalk
- ○ Petrol
- ○ Wet Stone
- ○ Mushroom
- ○ Damp Soil
- ○ Iron
- ○ Beetroot
- ○ Smoke
- ○ Tar

OAK/SPICE:

- ◯ Vanilla
- ◯ Clove
- ◯ Nutmeg
- ◯ Cinnamon
- ◯ Allspice
- ◯ Ginger
- ◯ White Pepper
- ◯ Caramel
- ◯ Smoke
- ◯ Toast
- ◯ Black Pepper

OTHER:

- ◯ Butter
- ◯ Butterscotch
- ◯ Cream
- ◯ Nut
- ◯ Honey
- ◯ Cocoa
- ◯ Bacon
- ◯ Iodine

Starting Your Exploration

Perhaps the best and most understandable way to approach your own wine education is to become familiar with the grape varieties used in winemaking. When learning how to cook, we learn first about the ingredients we use. We explore the differences among meats, fish, shellfish, vegetables, grains, spices, herbs, and the interplay of all these elements in creating a recipe. With wine, we can learn about the characteristics that grape varieties impart and then explore how various winemaking techniques—the "spice" of the process—affect the wines.

This chapter lists 60 or so grape varieties that encompass a broad range of styles and origins. Some of these grapes are common and some are esoteric. How do you make any sense of this array? We suggest starting with one grape. Find a bottle that appeals to you and have pen and paper at hand to record your sight-smell-taste impressions. Start by enjoying the wine, though, and the documentation will be easier.

Begin your exploration by checking off the familiar names and seeking out something new. We encourage you to write notes in this book. Discovering new wines or revisiting familiar favorites is more meaningful when you remember the context—where you were and who you were with.

If you try just one new wine a month, you'll know a dozen in a year's time and be much more comfortable when navigating a wine list or deciding what to buy for tonight's dinner. If you try one new wine a week, you'll be through

the entire list in just over a year and be way ahead of
nearly everyone you know in your wine knowledge and
tasting experience.

It's time to dive in, so head for your favorite restaurant or
retail shop and check off your first discovery today. To make
the experience even more fun and instructive, join with
friends to take the Diving Into Wine Challenge. Pick two,
four, six, or however many varieties then gather together
and taste them side by side. It's the easiest way to zero in on
your personal preferences.

White Wine Grapes

○ **Albariño/Alvarinho** (al-ba-REEN-yo) Aromatic grape with
floral and tangerine tones grown in Galicia in NW Spain
and the Minho of northern Portugal.

DATE & PLACE: _____

NOTES: _____

_____

_____

○ **Arneis** (are-NAYS) A distinctive variety of northern Italy's
Piedmont region. It often shows lively citrus and
tropical fruit nuances with hints of almond and subtle
herb tones.

DATE & PLACE: _____

NOTES: _____

_____

_____

○ **Assyrtiko** (ah-SEER-tee-koh) Exceptional Greek grape yielding concentrated citrus, peach, and tropical fruit character. Especially fine from the island of Santorini.

DATE & PLACE: _____

NOTES: _____

_____

_____

○ **Chardonnay** (SHAR-doe-nay) One of the great white wine grapes of the world, spanning many styles and character-istics based on regional differences and winemaking tech-niques. Often shows ripe apple, pear, citrus, and tropical fruits. Frequently oak aged, showing vanilla, cream, and baking spice tones as a result. Originally from Burgundy but widely grown in Champagne, Australia, the US, South America, South Africa, and elsewhere.

DATE & PLACE: _____

NOTES: _____

_____

_____

○ **Chenin Blanc** (shen-in BLAHNK) An overlooked grape with an impressive range of floral and apple/pear aromas. Most noted in France's Loire Valley where it makes sparkling (Saumur), bone dry (Savennières), off-dry (Vouvray), and sweet (Coteaux du Layon) styles. Also grown widely in South Africa, where it is sometimes called Steen.

DATE & PLACE: _____

NOTES: _____

_____

○ **Falanghina** (fal-an-GHEE-nah) An exotic and perfumed ancient variety grown mostly in southern Italy's Campania and surrounding regions. Best when young, Falanghina combines floral, lemon, tangerine, and tropical fruit elements in an appealing and dry style.

DATE & PLACE: _____

NOTES: _____

_____

_____

○ **Fumé Blanc**—See **Sauvignon Blanc**

○ **Furmint** (FOOR-mint) Spicy, appley grape best known for Tokaji Aszu dessert wines in Hungary. Makes fiery, characterful dry wines as well.

DATE & PLACE: _____

NOTES: _____

_____

_____

○ **Gewürztraminer** (geh-VUERTZ-tra-mee-ner) Powerfully aromatic grape with intense, floral, lychee, tropical fruit, pine, and honey character. Made in dry to sweet styles. Best known from Alsace in France. Also from Germany, northern Italy, Washington, Oregon, California, New Zealand, and Australia.

DATE & PLACE: _____

NOTES: _____

_____

_____

○ **Grüner Veltliner** (groo-ner velt-LEEN-er) Aromatic variety with peach and melon fruit plus green herb, floral, and white pepper nuances. Generally dry, but some sweet styles are made. Almost always from Austria.

DATE & PLACE: _____

NOTES: _____

_____

_____

○ **Macabeo/Viura** (mak-a-BAY-oh/vee-OOR-ah) Productive variety of northern Spain. As Viura, it makes the whites of Rioja. As Macabeo it is widely used in the blend for sparkling Cava wines.

DATE & PLACE: _____

NOTES: _____

_____

_____

○ **Malvasia/Malmsey** (mal-vah-ZEE-ah/MAHLM-zee) Ancient variety widely grown throughout Europe. Makes the rich, sweet Malmseys of Madeira and honeyed, exotic dessert wines in Italy and Greece. Often used as a blending partner to Trebbiano to add character to dry wines in central Italy.

DATE & PLACE: _____

NOTES: _____

_____

_____

○ **Muscadet/Melon de Bourgogne** (MOOSE-kah-day/
  may-lone deh boor-GON-yeh) Creates fresh, crisp, lemony
  wines often with hints of fresh-bread yeastiness from the
  Pays Nantais of western France.

  DATE & PLACE: _____

  NOTES: _____

  _____

  _____

○ **Muscat/Moscato** (MOOSE-kaht/moe-SCOTT-oh) Aromatic
  variety with gardenia/floral, lime, and tropical fruit
  character. Best known for sweet and fizzy styles in
  northern Italy, sweet styles in southern France, and a
  dry style in Alsace.

  DATE & PLACE: _____

  NOTES: _____

  _____

  _____

○ **Pinot Blanc** (pee-no BLAHNK) The pale-skinned version
  of the Pinot family, makes a medium-bodied aromatic
  white with apple and peach hints and a refreshing
  minerality. Widely grown in Alsace in France, in
  northern Italy as Pinot Bianco, and in Germany and
  Austria where it is called Weissburgunder.

  DATE & PLACE: _____

  NOTES: _____

  _____

  _____

○ **Pinot Gris/Grigio** (pee-no GREE/GREE-jee-oh) The pink-skinned member of the Pinot family, often cropped at high yields to make the popular Pinot Grigio of northern Italy. Can make rich, creamy-textured wines with peach and truffle notes in Alsace. Now widely planted in the western US as well.

DATE & PLACE: _____

NOTES: _____

_____

_____

○ **Riesling** (REES-ling) Ranks with Chardonnay as the world's greatest white wine grapes. Highly aromatic with apple, citrus, peach, honey, flower, and spice nuances. Made in all styles from bone dry to voluptuously sweet. Has great aging potential. At its consistent best in Germany. Glorious renditions are made in Alsace and Austria as well as the Clare and Eden Valleys of South Australia.

DATE & PLACE: _____

NOTES: _____

_____

_____

○ **Roussanne** (ROO-sahn) A widely-used variety in the Rhône Valley of France. It provides peach, apricot and tropical fruit character, herbal nuances, and a rich texture to its wines. Plus, it develops a lovely, honeyed, nutty complexity from age. Generally blended with Marsanne in the northern Rhône, it makes the whites of Hermitage, Crozes-Hermitage, and St. Joseph. In the southern Rhône, it is used in Châteauneuf-du-Pape Blanc. It is occasionally grown in the Languedoc and Savoie of France as well as the Central Coast of California.

DATE & PLACE: _____

NOTES: _____

_____

_____

○ **Sauvignon Blanc/Fumé Blanc** (SO-vin-yawn BLAHNK/ FOO-may BLAHNK) Aromatic variety known for its grassy, herbal, sometimes flinty character with tart citrus and melon fruits. At its best as Sancerre and Pouilly Fumé in the Loire. It is more intense and assertive from Marlborough in New Zealand and the Casablanca Valley in Chile. Widely planted in Bordeaux, South Africa, and California as well.

DATE & PLACE: _____

NOTES: _____

_____

_____

○ **Sémillon** (SEH-mee-yone) A blending partner for Sauvignon Blanc in the Graves of Bordeaux where it adds a peachy, "waxy" character to the wine. Susceptible to noble rot and thus makes exceptional dessert wine in Sauternes. Makes characterful, ageable whites in Australia's Hunter Valley and in South Africa.

DATE & PLACE: _____

NOTES: _____

_____

○ **Seyval Blanc** (say-vahl BLANHK) A French/American hybrid that endures the harsh winters in the northern US. Makes a crisp, mildly aromatic white with lemon/lime fruit in dry to lightly sweet styles.

DATE & PLACE: _____

NOTES: _____

_____

_____

○ **Silvaner/Sylvaner** (SIL-von-er) Makes crisp, earthy, minerally, and sometimes perfumed wines with apple and citrus fruit character. Its finest renditions are made in Germany's Franconia and in France's Alsace.

DATE & PLACE: _____

NOTES: _____

_____

_____

○ **Torrontés** (tore-ron-TESS) Aromatic variety widely grown in northern Argentina's Salta region. Best when fresh and expressing vivid citrus and melon fruits and enchanting floral tones.

DATE & PLACE: _____

NOTES: _____

_____

_____

○ **Trebbiano/Ugni Blanc** (treb-ee-YAH-no/OON-yee blahnk)
Workhorse variety providing large volumes of relatively
simple but clean white wine with lemon and almond
hints. Often blended with the more characterful Malva-
sia in Italy, especially in Tuscany and in Orvieto wines
from Umbria. As Ugni Blanc, it makes crisp whites in
the Côte de Gascogne of southern France. Ugni Blanc is
also used for distilling into Cognac and Armagnac.

DATE & PLACE: _____

NOTES: _____

_____

_____

○ **Verdejo** (vair-DAY-ho) Aromatic variety that shows floral,
ripe peach, orange, and tangerine characteristics. Grown
primarily in Rueda in Central Spain.

DATE & PLACE: _____

NOTES: _____

_____

_____

○ **Verdelho** (vair-DELL-ho) An overlooked white grape that
makes aromatic, full-bodied wines with citrus and
tropical fruit tones in Australia. Also grown in Madeira
where it usually makes an off-dry style.

DATE & PLACE: _____

NOTES: _____

_____

_____

○ **Verdicchio** (vair-DEE-kee-oh) Makes the noted lemony-fresh, crisp, and dry white of the Marches on the Adriatic coast of Italy. A classic companion for seafood.

DATE & PLACE: _____

NOTES: _____

_____

_____

○ **Vermentino** (vair-men-TEE-no) Aromatic grape that makes characterful, floral, and peachy whites on the island of Sardinia. Also known as Rolle in southern France where it is used as a blending variety.

DATE & PLACE: _____

NOTES: _____

_____

_____

○ **Vernaccia** (vair-NOTCH-ee-yah) In Tuscany's San Gimignano, it makes flavorful dry whites with hints of peach and lemon peel, plus sometimes pungent herb and roasted nut tones. Confusingly, the Vernaccia name is used for different grapes in other Italian regions, but San Gimignano's is most common.

DATE & PLACE: _____

NOTES: _____

_____

_____

○ **Viognier** (VEE-own-yay) Powerful, heady, aromatic white grape with its history in Condrieu of the northern Rhône. Peach, apricot, and violet perfume mark Viognier. Now planted in southern France's Languedoc as well as California, Australia, Chile, and New Zealand.

DATE & PLACE: _____

NOTES: _____

_____

_____

∾

You may have difficulty discerning which grape varieties are used in some wines. In traditional Old World winegrowing regions, wines are commonly labeled by their geographic origin, rather than the grape variety. Historically, consumers bought the wines from Gevrey-Chambertin, Montrachet, Barolo, and so forth, because those were the best wines available. They did not know the wines were made from Pinot Noir (Gevrey), Chardonnay (Montrachet), or Nebbiolo (Barolo). Winemakers in these areas feel that, with centuries of experience, it is the land, not the grape, that makes the difference. Thus, the geography-based appellations have endured.

That tradition leaves enthusiastic "divers" with a bit of homework. Invest in a good wine reference book or use the Internet. A quick search tells you that wines labeled Naoussa are made from Xynomavro and those labeled Hermitage are made from Syrah. It's a fun search, because the stories behind wine make them all the more intriguing, especially when you realize that winelovers hundreds of years ago were drinking wines from the same vineyards used today.

Red Wine Grapes

○ **Agiorgitiko** (ah-hee-yor-EE-tee-koh) Characterful variety grown in Nemea in Greece, sometimes anglicized to St. George. Offers blackberry and cherry fruit plus spicy complexity. The best versions can age well.

DATE & PLACE: _____

NOTES: _____

_____

_____

○ **Aglianico** (al-ee-ON-ee-koh) Creates powerful and ageable, if often rustic, red wines in Italy's Campania and Basilicata regions. Shows bold red and black fruits at its best in Taurasi and Aglianico del Vulture.

DATE & PLACE: _____

NOTES: _____

_____

_____

○ **Barbera** (bar-BEAR-ah) Juicy and lively variety widely grown in northern Italy. Plummy fruit and bright acidity makes it a versatile food companion. New World sources are California and Argentina.

DATE & PLACE: _____

NOTES: _____

_____

_____

○ **Blaufränkisch** (blau-FRANK-ish) An overlooked variety that makes medium-bodied, earthy, substantial red wines with black and red fruit character in Austria and Hungary. Known as Lemberger or Blue Franc in Washington State.

DATE & PLACE: _____

NOTES: _____

_____

_____

○ **Cabernet Franc** (CAB-air-nay FRAHNK) Creates supple, smooth reds with black cherry, graphite, and green pepper elements. Used in Bordeaux red blends and in the Loire Valley for Chinon, Bourgueil, etc. Widely planted in the US as a blending partner for Cabernet Sauvignon and Merlot wines.

DATE & PLACE: _____

NOTES: _____

_____

_____

○ **Cabernet Sauvignon** (CAB-air-nay SO-veen-yawn) A great red wine grape planted with success throughout the world. Exhibits powerful blackcurrant and blackberry fruit with deep, herbal, earthy, mint, and spicy nuances. Often benefits from several years of barrel and bottle aging. Grown in Bordeaux, California, Australia, South America, and South Africa with fine results.

CABERNET SAUVIGNON, CONTINUED

DATE & PLACE: _____

NOTES: _____

_____

_____

○ **Carignan/Carineña** (CAR-in-yawn/car-in-YAY-nah)
Workhorse Spanish variety now widely grown in southern France as well as northern Spain. Yields black fruity,
chunky, but simple wines on its own, thus normally
blended with more characterful varieties. Widely used
in Corbières and Côtes du Roussillon wines.

DATE & PLACE: _____

NOTES: _____

_____

_____

○ **Carmenère** (CAR-men-air) Originally from Bordeaux,
now widely grown in Chile where it makes rich, herbal,
black fruity red wines with hints of roasted coffee.

DATE & PLACE: _____

NOTES: _____

_____

_____

○ **Corvina** (core-VEE-nah) The most characterful grape used in the blend for Valpolicella, Bardolino, and Amarone in Italy's Veneto. It provides juicy, cherry fruit with almond hints.

DATE & PLACE: _____

NOTES: _____

_____

_____

○ **Dolcetto** (dole-CHET-toe) Deeply colored, juicy variety from Piedmont in northern Italy. Combines black fruits with snappy herb and peppery nuances.

DATE & PLACE: _____

NOTES: _____

_____

_____

○ **Gamay** (gam-MAY) The grape of Beaujolais where it creates pure, vibrant, juicy and gulpable wines with lots of strawberry and cherry fruits and floral hints.

DATE & PLACE: _____

NOTES: _____

_____

_____

○ **Grenache/Garnacha** (gren-AAHSH/Gar-NOTCH-ah) Fine grape of Spanish origin most noted in the southern Rhône areas of Châteauneuf-du-Pape and Gigondas where it makes heady reds with luscious strawberry jam-like fruit. Grown throughout southern France and much of northern Spain. Shows great potential in South Australia and California.

DATE & PLACE: _____

NOTES: _____

_____

_____

○ **Lambrusco** (lam-BREW-sko) Workhorse variety of Emilia-Romagna in northern Italy where it makes fizzy, sweet reds for the mass market. Dry versions combine black and red fruits and can be quite concentrated. It's a great grape to pair with proscuitto and other charcuterie.

DATE & PLACE: _____

NOTES: _____

_____

_____

○ **Malbec** (MAL-beck) A minor blending variety in Bordeaux taken to Argentina where it flourishes in the dry climate and high-altitude vineyards. The best versions are deeply colored, plummy, and spicy. Frequently oak aged and capable of cellaring for a few years.

Malbec, continued

Date & Place: _____

Notes: _____

_____

_____

○ **Mencía** (men-THEE-ah) This characteristic variety, known as Jaen in Portugal, comes to us primarily from northern Spain, most famously in Bierzo, where it is the predominant red grape. The best examples can have a floral and earthy complexity, a combination of red and black fruits, plus an appetizing herbal/peppery element and a lively, bracing acidity.

Date & Place: _____

Notes: _____

_____

_____

○ **Merlot** (mer-LOW) The most widely planted grape in Bordeaux, where it comprises the bulk of most AOC Bordeaux and Bordeaux Supérieur blends, offering luscious black cherry fruit to the mix. Makes its finest wines in Pomerol and St. Emilion. Grown successfully in Italy, Spain, Switzerland, California, Washingon State, Argentina, Chile, South Africa, Australia, and New Zealand.

Date & Place: _____

Notes: _____

_____

_____

○ **Montepulciano** (mon-tay-pull-chee-AH-no) Grape of considerable potential when yields are limited and the spicy, blackberry fruit is evident. Grown throughout southern Italy but especially successful in Marches (as Rosso Conero and Conero DOCG) and Abruzzo.

DATE & PLACE: _____

NOTES: _____

_____

_____

○ **Mourvèdre/Monastrell/Mataro** (more-VED-rr/ MOAN-a-strel/ma-TAR-oh) Powerful, sometimes pungent red originally from Spain but important in Provence for Bandol and as a component variety in Rhône blends. Yields rich and powerful reds as Monastrell in Jumilla, Alicante, and other Mediterranean coastal areas of Spain. Also grown in California and Australia.

DATE & PLACE: _____

NOTES: _____

_____

_____

○ **Nebbiolo** (nebb-ee-OH-low) The great grape of Barolo and Barbaresco in Italy's Piedmont. Yields wines of great dimension with red fruits, floral, tea, sandalwood, "forest floor," and anise notes. Benefits from long aging to allow its substantial tannins to soften.

DATE & PLACE: _____

NOTES: _____

_____

○ **Nero d'Avola** (nair-oh DAHV-o-la) An up-and-coming variety widely planted in Sicily. It combines black and red fruit elements with intriguing herb and spice nuances.

DATE & PLACE: _____

NOTES: _____

_____

_____

○ **Negroamaro** (NEG-ro-ah-MAHR-oh) The predominant grape in southern Italy's Apulia region. Provides rich, powerful, and often rustic but appealingly hearty reds with blackberry and blackcurrant fruits.

DATE & PLACE: _____

NOTES: _____

_____

_____

○ **Petite Sirah** (peh-TEET seer-ah) Originally the Durif of southern France, now a cult favorite in California where it creates heady, powerful, black fruity, and tannic reds.

DATE & PLACE: _____

NOTES: _____

_____

_____

○ **Pinot Noir** (pee-no NWAHR) The great red grape of Burgundy where its best versions demonstrate memorable breadth and nuance, combining fruit, floral, herb, and spice notes with a delicacy unmatched by other varieties. Frequently planted in the Languedoc of southern France, in northern Italy as Pinot Nero and in Germany as Spätburgunder. Successfully grown in Oregon, California, and in cooler areas of Australia, New Zealand, Chile, and South Africa.

DATE & PLACE: _____

NOTES: _____

_____

_____

○ **Pinotage** (pee-no-TAHJ) South African crossing of Pinot Noir and Cinsault that at its best yields black fruity reds with a wild herbal and often smoky component.

DATE & PLACE: _____

NOTES: _____

_____

_____

○ **Sangiovese** (san-jee-oh-VAY-zeh) The fine grape of Tuscany and central Italy. The predominant grape in Chianti, Brunello di Montalcino, and Morellino di Scansano wines. Pure red cherry style when young that can develop attractive earthy richness and fabulous dried fruit, herb, and cocoa complexity when aged.

Sangiovese, continued

Date & Place: _____

Notes: _____

_____

_____

○ **Syrah/Shiraz** (see-RAH/sheer-AHZ) Clearly one of the greatest red grapes. Creates long-aging wines with blackberry, blackcurrant, and plum fruits plus smoky spice in the northern Rhône. It is widely grown as well in the southern Rhône and throughout the broad sweep of Languedoc-Roussillon vineyards on the Mediterranean coast of France. Amenable to many climes, it is grown with great success as Shiraz in Australia and does well in Washington, California, South Africa, Chile, and Argentina.

Date & Place: _____

Notes: _____

_____

_____

○ **Tannat** (tah-NATT) A grape of Madiran in southern France noted for its fierce tannins and long aging. Softer, more user-friendly versions are now produced in Uruguay.

Date & Place: _____

Notes: _____

_____

_____

○ **Tempranillo** (temp-rah-NEE-oh) A grape synonymous with northern and central Spain. It is the predominant grape in many red Rioja blends offering pure red cherry fruit. Known as Tinto Fino in Ribera del Duero, Cencibel in La Mancha, Tinta Roriz or Aragonez in Portugal, it is successfully grown throughout Iberia. Shows promise in Washington State as well.

DATE & PLACE: _____

NOTES: _____

_____

_____

○ **Touriga Nacional** (tour-EE-gah nass-ee-oh-NAL) Yields, deeply colored, powerful, black fruity wines in Portugal. Not only is it the most important grape for Port production, it also is the base for many dry reds from the Douro and further south in Dão.

DATE & PLACE: _____

NOTES: _____

_____

_____

○ **Xynomavro** (ksee-NO-mav-ro) A variety grown in northern Greece's Macedonia region, particularly in Naoussa, where it yields often impressive, perfumed and nuanced, if tannic, wines with pure cherry fruit.

DATE & PLACE: _____

NOTES: _____

_____

_____

○ **Zinfandel** (ZIN-fen-dell) California's distinctive adopted
   grape. DNA evidence reveals that it is the same as
   the Crljenak grape of Croatia and a sibling of Italy's
   Primitivo. Highly productive if not controlled,
   Zinfandel can combine cranberry and blackberry fruit
   characteristics with a wild, woodsy nuance.

DATE & PLACE: _____

NOTES: _____

_____

_____

What Glass to Use

Glassware is an important part of any table setting, adding a transparent, reflective, vertical dimension that catches the eye. When filled with a brilliantly colored wine, good stemware is a marvelous marriage of form and function.

A mind-boggling range of shapes and styles of glassware is available from any number of sources. From our perspective, though, too many of the vessels marketed as wine glasses do little to enhance, and in fact, often diminish the winetasting experience.

The essential ingredients for functional stemware are size, proportion, shape, and color.

The size of the bowl should be large enough, if filled 1/3 to 1/2 of its capacity, to allow for sufficient room to swirl the wine and provide a generous, not excessive, portion for the drinker.

When you pick up the stem, is the bowl so large that it is top-heavy? If so, the proportions are wrong and could be the cause of many mishaps on your table linens.

The bowl of the glass should taper inward at the top. Without the tapering shape, it is very easy for your guests to slosh the wine on themselves and their neighbors as they swirl. The stem should be long enough for easy handling. Your hand can affect the temperature of the wine if it is too close to the bowl (that's why the glass should always be handled by the stem).

Etched, cut, or colored stemware can be a beautiful addition to the table, but colorings or markings detract from the sensory experience of the wine tasting, making it impossible to view the hue and clarity of the wine. Also, the thinner the glass the better for viewing and tasting. Distortions from thick glass can skew the view. You want to see the wine, not the glass!

White wine glasses are smaller than those for reds. An all-purpose red wine glass, however, can handle the job for most drinkers.

Champagne and sparkling wines show their bubbly best in a tulip or flute, not in those saucers that are best used for dessert.

Use a smaller version of the white wine glass for sweet dessert wines, Port, and Madiera. Distillers around the world prefer a small bowl with a straight narrow opening to concentrate and focus the ethereal scents of Cognac, Armagnac, Scotch, Calvados, and brandies.

Here is a list of the most common glass shapes, their capacities, and uses.

 Port/Sherry/Dessert Wine Glass: The capacity of this glass ranges from 4 to 8 ounces (120 to 240 ml) and is best for sweet or fortified wines like Port, Sherry, and Madeira, where the standard portion is smaller.

 **Champagne Flute:** The best shape for enjoying Champagne or other sparkling wines is tall and narrow. Capacity generally ranges from 6 to 10 ounces (180 to 300 ml) and allows you to visually appreciate the steady flow of bubbles.

 **White Wine Glass:** This elegant, tapered bowl generally has a capacity ranging from 11 to 14 ounces (325 to 420 ml). While this glass is a good choice for most white wines, the finest full-bodied Chardonnays show well in a Burgundy shape.

 **Burgundy Glass:** The broad bowl and 22 to 28 ounce (650 to 830 ml) capacity allow the delicate aromas of Pinot Noir, Nebbiolo, Xynomavro, and other more delicate varieties to shine.

 **Bordeaux Glass:** The taller, more slender profile and large 20 to 28 ounce (600 to 830 ml) capacity is best for appreciating bold red grape varieties like Cabernet Sauvignon, Malbec, and Syrah.

You can enhance your wine enjoyment by selecting the best glass that your budget and usage habits permit. You can buy very expensive stemware, but might be afraid to use it for fear of breakage. There is no point in purchasing wine glasses unless you are willing to use them!

Keep these thoughts in mind when you shop for stemware:

- Look for the tapered form shared by all the illustrated glass shapes. This shape is essential for swirling the wine and releasing the aromas that have been trapped in the bottle.

- What sort of wines do you drink most frequently? Buy the shape you will use most often. For example, if your wine preferences lean toward Bordeaux (Cabernet Sauvignon) or Burgundy (Pinot Noir) on a regular basis, invest in a slightly larger bowl to enjoy these wines fully.

- Do you run every glass through the dishwasher? If so, select a sturdier glass. If you are willing to hand-wash glasses, you can look at finer (and more expensive) crystal offerings.

- Does the glass feel comfortable in your hand? Is the stem too short or long for you? Does it seem top-heavy? If it is top-heavy when empty, it will be worse when it is full.

- Look at the thickness of the rim. Rolled rims tend to dribble when used. Thinner rims offer a more elegant appearance as well as fewer drips down the glass.

The perfect glass for you should fit your hand, feel balanced, and enhance your appreciation of the appearance, aroma, and taste of the wine.

Finally, once you have invested in glasses, keep your stemware spotlessly clean and odor-free. Strong detergent residue can ruin the tasting experience. Thoroughly rinse and polish your stemware to maximize wine appreciation. Use a lint-free cloth for the best sheen or in a pinch try a clean coffee filter on still damp stemware (yes, it really works).

Wine & Food

 Part of the joy of wine is pairing it with food. Throughout the world, wine traditions have evolved concomitantly with culinary traditions. When the match is right, the wine tastes better, the food tastes better, and each bite allows you to revel in the intricate interplay of flavors and textures.

That said, the "perfect match" is very elusive and there are many wine choices that serve perfectly well with a wide variety of dishes. Here are a few guidelines, however, that will enhance your wine and food combinations:

Select wines, regardless of color, to match the power of the food. In other words, if you have light-bodied foods, pick a light-bodied wine. If you have hearty, full-flavored foods, select a full-bodied wine.

Think about the dominant characteristics of the dish you are preparing in relation to what the human palate perceives. The primary components people can taste are sweet, salty, bitter, sour, and umami (savory). We won't delve into umami deeply, but it is a sensation exemplified by savory tastes like broth, aged cheese, and so forth.

If your dish is high in acid—lemon juice and tomato sauce are two common elements—choose a wine with high acid to match.

If your recipe is salty—cured meats or smoked fish, for example—pair with wines that have both high acidity and a degree of sweetness, such as Champagne and sparkling wine.

If your dish has sweet components (and lots of dishes do, such as Asian dishes, fruit sauces or marinades, barbeque sauces, onions, carrots), select a wine with enough sweet elements to match the sweetness of the dish.

Use tannic wines to pair with dishes that have significant fat components (grilled steaks or burgers, for instance).

Avoid tannic wines with fish oils—they will make the dish seem aggressively fishy.

Be careful with spicy dishes and wines with high alcohol. Alcohol fans the flames and make the dish seem hotter (if you like heat—go for it!). Wines with low alcohol and/or residual sugar tame the heat.

What follows is a list of wine suggestions for various foods. These are guidelines, not rules! Keep in mind that the preparations of any recipe can vary greatly, depending on the intensity and freshness of ingredients, and the cook's preference for levels of spicing. Nonetheless, these wines are worth considering if you are preparing the dish.

ASIAN FOODS: This category is broad, but Thai, Chinese, Japanese, and Vietnamese recipes often have significant sweet components so wines with inherent sweetness do well. Try German or US Riesling, Champagne or sparkling wine, or Moscato d'Asti from Italy. Don't forget to consider a fine Junmai Ginjo Sake as well.

ASPARAGUS: A difficult match for most wines, but is easier if you grill the asparagus. Try a Sauvignon Blanc from Sancerre or Pouilly-Fumé; or a Grüner Veltliner from Austria.

BARBEQUE: Pick your wine based on the sauce type. Sweet/sour styles do very well with richer rosé wines from Syrah, Malbec, or Zinfandel. Tangy/high vinegar sauces can pair with red Zinfandel, Garnacha from Spain, Barbera from Italy, Agiorgitiko from Greece. If the sauce is spicy, select a lower alcohol alternative.

BEEF: Although preparations are diverse, beef is a natural with Cabernet Sauvignon wines, whether from Bordeaux, Chile, Argentina, South Africa, the US, or elsewhere. Merlot, Malbec, and Syrah are all good alternatives. In fact, almost any full-flavored red can do well. Pick your favorite and enjoy. Grilled steaks do particularly well with young red Bordeaux or California Cabernet Sauvignons: "a slab and a cab," as one friend in wine so aptly stated. Beef Bourguignon invites bringing out your best aged wine to pair with the earthy richness of the dish. Braised beef dishes, like slow cooked short ribs, marry beautifully with Petite Sirahs from California, Shiraz/Cabernet blends from Australia, or Merlots from the coastal areas of Tuscany.

CHEESE: There are so many cheeses that it's impossible to make a single recommendation. Generally, however, white wines go better with more cheeses than reds. Here are some additional recommendations:

Blue cheeses: Wines with sweetness can be stars! Try German Riesling Auslese, Beerenauslese or Trockenbeerenauslese; French Sauternes or Coteaux du Layon; Hungarian Tokaji; Ruby, Tawny or Vintage Port; Sweet Cream Sherries.

Goat cheeses: Sancerre and Pouilly-Fumé are classics, and deservedly so. Also New Zealand Sauvignon Blanc, Vernaccia di San Gimignano, and other crisp, pungent whites.

Hard, aged cheeses: Champagne works well, also Dry Grand Cru Rieslings or Pinot Gris from Alsace. For reds, Amarone or Chianti Classico Riserva from Italy.

Mild, semi-soft cheeses: The most wine friendly cheeses. Try an unoaked Chardonnay from California or Australia, a Mâcon-Villages from France, or Arneis from Italy. Australian Shiraz pairs well with a mild, nutty Swiss as do Washington Syrah or California Merlot.

Ripened cheeses: Milder versions like Brie and Camembert pair well with light, non-tannic reds like Beaujolais or Barbera. Strong styles like Epoisses overwhelm most wines. Try a late harvest Pinot Gris or Gewurztraminer from Alsace.

CHICKEN: Wine choices depend on the preparation. Simple roasted chicken is delicious with full-flavored whites like California Chardonnay, white Côtes du Rhône or Meursault from France; Assyrtiko from Greece; reds like Pinot Noir, Red Rioja, Côtes du Rhône, and Argentine Malbec. Coq au Vin is a fabulous dish for an aged red, especially from Burgundy or Bordeaux.

DESSERTS: There are so many varied sweets in the culinary world that it would take a separate volume to cover them all. The primary criterion for matching desserts with dessert wines is to be certain that the sweetness of the wine is greater than the sweetness of the dish. Otherwise, even a fine and expensive wine will seem thin and acidic.

DUCK: Roast duck (without a fruit glaze or sauce) is classic with Pinot Noir from pretty much anywhere. Duck is a good match with younger red Bordeaux or Chinon from the Loire Valley.

FISH AND SHELLFISH: The sheer variety of fish and preparation make universal recommendations difficult.

Flaky white fish: Light fish, like sole or cod do well with similarly light-bodied whites like Soave, Bordeaux Blanc, Verdicchio, and Orvieto from Italy or Albariño from Spain.

Steak-like fish: Tuna, swordfish, and other steak-like fish pair with full bodied whites like Premier Cru Chablis or white Burgundy. Vermentino from Italy, Assyrtiko from Greece, Roussanne from California or France also work.

Salmon: Pinot Gris from Alsace in France or the Pacific Northwest is a great choice. Dry Rosés are wonderful and full bodied whites like Chardonnay (the less oak the better) and New Zealand Sauvignon Blanc can do well. Grilled or broiled salmon is good with red wines like Zinfandel, Côtes du Rhône, or Argentine Malbec.

Shellfish: Oysters are classic with Muscadet from the Loire, crisp Chablis, light Sauvignon Blanc, or very dry Champagne. Shrimp can be fine when cooked and served with dry Sherry, dry Riesling, or Sauvignon Blanc. (The standard sweet shrimp cocktail sauce defeats most wines.) Lobster with drawn butter is sensationally good with a luscious, oaked Chardonnay from California or Australia.

HAM AND OTHER SMOKED MEATS: Salt is the key element here. Off-dry whites like Riesling Kabinett or Spätlese from Germany, Vouvray, or a fat Alsace Pinot Gris from France. Champagne and other bubblies can work well.

INDIAN CURRIES: The sweet/hot spice mix of most curries does well with Champagne or sparkling wine, German Rieslings, California or South African Chenin Blanc, or Albariño from Spain for whites. Youthful Rhône reds like Gigondas or Vacqueyras are good, as are Dolcetto from Italy, Monastrell from Spain or Dão from Portugal.

LAMB: An aged California Cabernet Sauvignon matches the gamey/earthy tones of roast lamb beautifully. Aged red Bordeaux or Carmenère from Chile are good, as are Ribera del Duero from Spain or Cabernet Sauvignon from South Africa.

LIVER: Youthful reds work best. Try a young Bordeaux Supérieur or St. Emilion, a Cru Beaujolais or a Côtes du Ventoux from France, Montepulciano d'Abruzzo, Barbera or Teroldego from Italy.

NUTS (ALMONDS, HAZELNUTS, MACADAMIAS): Dry Sherry is a classic, but a bit of a shock to the American palate. Try a Fino, Manzanilla, or Amontillado.

PAELLA: Although paella varies with the chef, it is always a richly flavored and textured dish. Try Tempranillo based wines from Rioja in Spain, McLaren Vale Grenache from Australia, or a Mourvédre based red from Bandol in France for chicken and sausage-based recipes. Seafood-based paella can pair well with Riesling or Grüner Veltliner from Austria, Verdejo from Spain, or Sauvignon Blanc from New Zealand.

PASTA: Pasta dishes take on the character of the sauce. Here are some recommendations for common pasta preparations:

Alfredo Sauce: The lavish cream and cheese combo needs a vibrant, edgy wine to cut through it. Try Sangiovese from Tuscany or Emilia-Romagna, Tempranillo from Spain for reds; Vernaccia di San Gimignano, Greco di Tufo, or Sicilian Inzolia for whites.

Lasagne: Try a rich-textured wine to match the richness of the dish. Brunello di Montalcino, Chianti Riserva, or Nebbiolo from Italy; Zinfandel or Barbera from California; Bierzo from Spain and Bandol from France are all possibilities.

Pesto: The classic sauce of basil, garlic, and pine nuts pairs well with whites like Pinot Grigio, Vermentino, or Cortese from northern Italy. Sauvignon Blancs from California or New Zealand are other possibilities.

Seafood: Many seafood pasta recipes incorporate white wine, garlic, and Mediterranean herbs. Try a Falanghina or Vernaccia from Italy, a Roussanne from France or a Viura from Rioja in Spain.

Spaghetti and Meatballs with Marinara: An Italo-American classic that pairs well with a wide range of Italian reds. Try Chianti, Salice Salentino, Barbera, Dolcetto, Aglianico, or Valpolicella.

PIZZA: An easy match for a wide range of Italian reds—try something unusual! California Zinfandel, Jumilla from Spain, Pinotage from South Africa, Douro reds from Portugal, and Bonarda from Argentina are all worth trying.

PORK: The relatively neutral flavor of pork rewards red or white wines. As with chicken, the preparation is key. California Chardonnay or Australian Semillon/Chardonnay, Oregon Pinot Gris, Verdelho from Australia for whites. Youthful reds work well, also. Pinot Noir from New Zealand, Dolcetto from Italy, Merlot from California, Grenache from Australia. Dry rosés from southern France or Spain are delicious with grilled pork.

RISOTTO: The creamy texture of risotto needs a full-textured wine. Arneis, Fiano, Greco, or Falanghina from Italy for whites. Mushroom risotto is classic with fine Barolo and Barbaresco. Seafood or spring vegetable risottos work well with Pinot Blanc, Côtes du Rhône Blanc, or the same Italian whites.

SAUSAGES: Reds with acid and tannin to parry the fatty style of bratwurst or Italian sausages—young Chianti, Valpolicella, Zinfandel, Tempranillo (without much oak).

Chicken or turkey sausages can pair well with aromatic whites like Riesling from Germany or Austria. The sparkling sweetness of Italy's Moscato d'Asti works well with chicken-apple or other subtly sweet sausages.

SOUP: There is some difficulty in matching liquids with other liquids, especially at different temperatures, but there are some good choices. Broth-based soups pair well with dry Sherries and Madeiras, especially when there is a dollop of the wine in the broth. Cream-based soups can do well with richly textured whites.

TURKEY: The subtle sweetness of turkey rewards pairing with subtly sweet wines like Riesling, Pinot Gris, Gewurztraminer and Chenin Blanc wines from France (Vouvray) and South Africa. Rich reds like Côtes du Rhône, Corbières, and Minervois from France; Alicante or Utiel-Requena from Spain ; or Primitivo from Italy (aka Zinfandel) are good choices.

VEGETABLES: Roasting vegetables enhances the flavor and makes them more wine friendly. Try a Pinot Blanc from Alsace, a Pinot Gris from Oregon, or an Albariño from Spain for whites. Good red choices include Cru Beaujolais and Coteaux du Languedoc from France, Garnacha from Spain, or Pinot Noir from California.

VENISON/GAME MEATS: Break out your big reds—Côte Rôtie or Hermitage from France, Amarone or Sagrantino di Montefalco from Italy, Syrah from Washington or California, Shiraz from Australia, or Ribera del Duero from Spain.

What Temperature?

It only takes a bit of personal research to discover that the temperature at which you serve a wine can dramatically affect your appreciation of the beverage.

In my experience, way too much fine wine suffers because it is served too cold or too hot. Curiously, restaurants, which have more invested in wine and should arguably know better, are among the most common offenders when it comes to serving wines at inappropriate temperature levels.

If you're drinking a good white wine, do not overchill it. Excessively cold temperatures subdue the aromas of a fine wine and often numb the palate to the point where you can only recognize a cold liquid flowing over your tongue. If you're drinking swill, by all means chill it to near the freezing point. If, however, you've spent some serious money on a fine bottle, don't diminish your investment and bypass your senses.

Fine white wines should spend perhaps an hour in the refrigerator (down to 50-55°F/10-13°C or so) before serving, not the day or more that most wines seem to be subjected to.

The time-honored rule for red wines is to serve the bottle at room temperature. The temperature of most rooms in modern America is about ten degrees or more warmer that those of 18th or 19th century Europe, when that rule of thumb originated. Consequently, too much red wine is served too warm, accentuating the sharp, somewhat acetic elements that are present in virtually all wines and making the wine much less attractive than it would be if served a few degrees cooler.

If you are storing your red wines on the kitchen counter, on top of the refrigerator, or in some other warm setting, you might consider a cooler spot for them, or at least cool them down for 20 minutes or so before serving. You'll find the aromas are far more attractive and the flavors much richer and more sumptuous if you do.

Temperatures for Serving Wine

CHAMPAGNE AND SPARKLING WINES	43-50°F	(6-10°C)
LIGHT DRY WHITE WINES AND ROSÉS	45-50°F	(7-10°C)
RICH WHITES AND LIGHT REDS	50-55°F	(10-13°C)
MEDIUM-BODIED REDS	55-60°F	(13-15°C)
FULL-BODIED AND AGED REDS	60-65°F	(15-18°C)
RICH DESSERT WINES	50-60°F	(10-15°C)

Corks & Closures

Much misinformation surrounds the cork that seals a wine bottle. Questions about what to do with the cork when it is presented by your server at a restaurant confound virtually everyone who has been in that situation. Yet the tradition has quite practical roots.

The cork presentation ritual began as a way to guarantee the authenticity of the wine in the bottle. Prior to the 1960s, many wines were shipped to market in casks and bottled by the firm that purchased the wine. Because of this diverse upbringing, wines from the same source were quite variable. As estate bottling became more prevalent, the corks were embossed with the estate name and vintage thus confirming the authenticity of the wine.

It is not uncommon for corks, especially older corks, to be wet or dry or spongy, or for corks to break while opening. The longer a cork has remained in a bottle, the greater the likelihood it will lose its elasticity and appear misshapen when extracted. When you see mold on the top of the cork, it means you should wipe it off. It is common for wine bottles, especially those of European provenance, to develop mold under the capsule after a few years. The mold does not penetrate the seal created by the cork.

After all is said and done, it's best to ignore the cork and taste the wine. I have sampled delicious wines with wet corks, dry corks, moldy corks, and every other permutation of cork you can imagine. I never make a determination about a wine's condition without smelling and tasting the wine itself. There is simply no other way.

An unfortunate aspect of cork, however, is the presence of "corkiness," a chemical taint that imbues the wine with a musty, wet cardboard aroma and flavor—effectively ruining the wine. This taint is present in 2 to 10 percent of all cork finished bottles. It is not surprising that many producers have opted for alternate closures—plastic corks, screwcaps, and the like. Do not dismiss a wine because of its closure. Fine wines are bottled in all permutations in the modern wine world.

Decanting Wine

❧

 The practice of decanting a bottle of wine is a familiar one to those who know and love good wine. For the uninitiated, though, decanting seems to be a mystical rite, perhaps rooted in a long-forgotten religion, that brings forth feelings of awe, bewilderment, and sometimes fear.

The task of decanting a bottle of wine need not be shrouded in such mystery. It is, after all, only a simple process of pouring a liquid from one container to another.

There are two significant reasons for decanting. The first is to expose a wine to air. Young red wines (and whites too, for that matter) benefit from a good mixing with air. This "breathing" allows the sometimes harsh tannic elements present in a youthful red to soften, making the wine more pleasurable to consume.

As red wines age, though, this softening process takes place naturally within the bottle due to chemical changes in the wine. The result of these molecular changes is the residue or sediment one can observe in an older bottle of red wine. Removing the liquid from the now solid portion of an older wine is the second reason for decanting.

Which young red wines need decanting? Any full-bodied red that is less than four years old is a good candidate, including Cabernet Sauvignon, Syrah/Shiraz, Merlot, and their blended counterparts, as well as Italian reds like Barolo, Barbaresco, and Amarone.

How do you know which wines contain sediment? Easy—
you look at the bottle. Hold it up to the light and you'll see
a fine particulate matter settled on the bottom or side of the
bottle, depending on the position of the vessel during storage.

Red wines over five years old should be examined, and one
should expect to see some degree of sediment formation in
reds over a decade old.

Prior to decanting, set the bottle upright or at a sufficient
upward angle to let the sediment slowly settle to the bottom
of the bottle.

The hardware needed for decanting is a light source and a
scrupulously clean vessel in which to pour the wine. This
container can range from an elegant, cut crystal decanter to
something as mundane as an old, but well-washed, mayon-
naise jar.

Traditionally a candle is used as a light source. A flashlight
works as well, but at the expense of the romance of the
ritual. One can also simply hold the bottle up beneath a ceil-
ing light fixture. The task is to remove the liquid from the
solid—the degree of trappings and ritual is up to you.

A steady hand, however, is required for efficient decanting since excessive motion will roil up the fine particulates and undo in an instant what nature has taken years to create.

Follow these steps for successful decanting:

1   Open the wine with a minimum of movement.

2   Place the candle or other light source where you are able to pour the wine above it comfortably.

3   Gently pick up the bottle and pour the wine into the decanting vessel with the light source beneath the neck of the wine bottle, being careful not to scorch the neck of the bottle.

4   As you get to the bottom of the bottle, you will see a stream of fine sediment come to the neck followed by a more opaque, heavier sediment. The point at which you stop pouring is up to you. You can let the finest sediment flow into the decanter, it does not alter the taste as much as the larger chunks.

5   Stop pouring just before the heavier sediment reaches the neck of the bottle. If you're curious, pour the sediment into a glass and taste the difference between the clear liquid and the cloudy. Now you understand the reason for decanting.

The key to effective decanting is to move slowly and treat the wine gently. Once you begin pouring the wine into the decanter, do not stop until the process is completed. Otherwise, the movement of the fluid in the bottle will mix the wine with the sediment—exactly what we're trying to avoid.

Note that young wines with no signs of sediment do not require the light source or the gentle handling since you are not going to encounter any solid matter. Just pour the wine from the bottle into the decanter. It's amazing how much that slight oxygenation can alter the textural sensation of the wine.

Storing Wine: Bottles & Cellars

As the last stage of winemaking, wine is put into bottles and labeled. The bottles provide storage for the wine, making it easy to transport and pour. In your home or at a restaurant, wine is presented to you in bottles. Once you begin collecting wine, you'll need a place to keep the wine bottles in your home. Regardless of the size of your collection, that storage becomes your "wine cellar."

What Does Bottle Shape Mean?

There is a romantic aspect to wine that seems to pervade every facet of its production, storage and consumption. The romance surrounding winemaking also encompasses the vessels in which it is stored—from the earthen amphorae of ancient Greece to wooden barrels to the manifold styles of the modern wine bottle. The diversity of styles, origins, and ages of wine is reflected in the myriad of bottle shapes and label styles.

The precise reasons for bottle shape variations are unknown and probably rooted in glass-manufacturing capabilities of the early 1700s. At that time bottles and corks first consummated the happy marriage that allows wines to develop without exposure to air. Once established by tradition, though, bottle shapes become ingrained in regional wine-making to the point where they may be codified into law.

Thus, nearly all Bordeaux are bottled in the elegant, high-shouldered, slim-sided bordelaise bottle traditional in the Bordeaux region, while wines from Burgundy are placed in the familiar slope-shouldered bottle familiar to all wine buyers. These two shapes are the most widely-used and wineries throughout the world emulate the French tradition by bottling Merlot and Cabernet Sauvignon (Bordeaux grape varieties) in the high-shouldered Bordeaux bottle while Chardonnay and Pinot Noir (Burgundy grape varieties) are ensconced in the traditional slope-shouldered Burgundy shape.

There are, of course, many variations from this pattern. The tall, slender flute of Alsace is the required vessel for any bottle sold as Vin d'Alsace. The flute shape is also common among German and Austrian wines, as well as wines made from Teutonic grapes (Riesling, Gewürztraminer, and so forth) from other parts of the world.

In modern times, specially crafted bottles with distinctive profiles and sometimes heavy weights have become common, thus further clouding the already hazy waters of bottle shapes. These days, the bottle shape can reflect tradition or merely the winery's desire for a distinctive appearance.

Creating Your Own Wine Cellar

Part of the joy of wine is having a range of wine styles at hand in your home. At a whim, you can sample the exotic spice and perfume of Pinot Noir, the refreshing herbal crispness of Sauvignon Blanc, the opulent texture of a barrel-aged Chardonnay, or the subtle complexity of a fine Bordeaux.

You can indulge yourself in this fashion only if you have a place to store your wines. If you spend some money on good wines, it only seems appropriate to give them the best home possible within your dwelling.

But where is that place? In the linen closet? That rack over the stove? The cobwebbed corner of the basement?

Designing proper storage for the long term can be crucial to the life of the liquid asset in the bottle. Several elements ensure your investment will reach maturity in the intended condition: temperature, humidity, light, and vibration. Think of those dark, damp, cold underground cellars in Europe, conditions that no reasonable person would consider living under, but perfect for the long, slow aging of fine wines. While most American homes are lacking in these "amenities," you can create these conditions artificially.

Finding just the right resting place for those special bottles does require a little hunting, planning, and forethought. First, locate an area that keeps a fairly consistent year-round temperature, optimal is 55°F/13°C. A slow gradual seasonal change varying as high as 70°F/21°C or as low as 40°F/5°C is acceptable, as long as it is not a daily fluctuation. Stay away from any heat source. Insulate the space, if necessary, to keep that temperature continuum.

This space should be dark, void of any natural light, and away from any continuous artificial light. Stay away from any locale that has any vibration. Don't use the space under the stairs if you have kids pounding up and down for the next 15 years. Likewise, the closet next to your teenager's sound system would be an inappropriate location.

Ok, now that you've found the perfect space, let's look at what to do with it. Are you looking for a showcase display or just the basic storage facility? Several companies will design the optimum redwood racking system, for a price, of course. A good carpenter can erect any type of built-in racks to fit the space, or have fun and design your own.

Now, how big you build it is determined by the space available plus how many cases you expect to accumulate. How often do you drink a bottle—five times a week, just on the weekends, or only on special occasions? Let's figure this out, if you drink on average five bottles a week, that comes out to 260 bottles or 21.66 cases per year. Are you looking for wines to age for 5 years, 10 years, 20 years or more? If so, then you should have one-third to one-half of your cellar reserved for those long-term bottles, which leaves you about 11 cases of capacity for current consumption.

If you consume your weekly average, you will go through a case in a little over two weeks, so you are purchasing at least two cases a month. Adjust these numbers accordingly to fit your drinking habits.

One caveat, don't lock yourself too heavily into one particular style of wine or a single vintage. Everyone's taste changes over time and you may grow tired of that wine you so loved a couple of years ago. Nor do you want to find yourself with everything maturing at the same time, and needing to "drink-up." Vary your collection by wine and vintage and you will always have the perfect bottle to drink.

Giving your wine a good home is not just wine snobbery run amok. If you've invested time and money in selecting good wines, it only makes sense to care for them well.

However, most wine that is consumed is not as frail and delicate a beverage as the most ardent proponents of perfect storage systems contend, especially if you drink the wine within a few months of purchase. Wines can suffer abuse and still remain quite drinkable. They will, in all likelihood, be less attractive than they might have been. Scan your living space to find the best spot available and ensure that your wines are the best they can be.

What Makes Wines Different?

 The great puzzle for winelovers of all
levels is defining the variables that
result in such divergent products in
the glass. What are the reasons for the
variability and nuance of wine? Is it the
grape variety? The vineyard soil? The
climate? The barrel aging? The winemaker's methods?
"Yes," is the answer to these questions and more. Any and
all aspects of viticulture, vinification, and cellaring can
influence the character of a wine.

Producing wine of any sort has never been an easy task.
Producing fine wine, however, is an endeavor so fraught
with unknowns and uncontrollable variables it's a wonder
anyone bothers.

Fortunately for winelovers, there are many wine producers
as enamored with wine as the most avid consumer. These
men and women are devoted to creating the best wine they
can possibly make, regardless of the inherent challenges or
expense. It has been said the best way to make a million dol-
lars in the wine business is to start with 10 million. So with
this in mind, let's take a moment to consider the myriad
of decisions and obstacles vintners must face when they
decide, for whatever reason, to grow grapes that will
be transformed into fine wine.

In the Vineyard

All wine starts in the vineyard. A winemaker can only make great wine if given great grapes. There are many aspects to consider when one gets ready to plant a vineyard.

The choice of a grape variety for a particular vineyard is crucial, but not simple. Each variety has a number of clones that exhibit slightly different tastes and characteristics. Are you after a wine with aging capabilities or something for early consumption? A wine with great complexity or just simply gulpable? The proper selection of clones allows a winemaker to achieve a desired flavor profile.

The soil and microclimate determine the grape variety best suited for the vineyard location. The French have a single word that encapsulates the entire notion of microclimate:"terroir." A vintner must consider the composition and depth of the soil and know which grape varieties respond well to those conditions. The terroir of the vineyard takes into account many variables, including:

Topography–aspect, terrain, elevation

Geology–soil characteristics, bedrock structure

Hydrology–precipitation, drainage

Heat–temperature, latitude, sunshine, fog

Drainage is a key factor in any vineyard planning decision. The best wines come from grapes grown on well-drained soils that force the vines to send their roots deep to find water. Vines are like any plant. They do not like to have their "feet" wet all the time, but they still need to find hydration during the growing season. In dry areas vintners supplement with irrigation.

Vintners must also consider the aspect of the potential vineyard—sloping vineyards promote good drainage and offer better exposure to sunlight than flat sites. Is it in a frost-prone location? Is there a river or body of water to moderate the temperature? What is the direction of the prevailing wind and at what velocity or cycle does it blow? If it's a windy location, then small bush vines will withstand a howling gale. If it's a very humid location, vines must be trained high and be well spaced to allow lots of air circulation around the grape bunches to resist rot.

Also, since most vines planted in America are European vines, they must be grafted onto native American rootstocks to keep phylloxera at bay. Phylloxera is a North American root louse that loves to munch on the roots of vitis vinifera vines (the classic wine grape varieties—Chardonnay, Cabernet Sauvignon, Pinot Noir, etc.). Thus, a new vineyard must not only be planted with the right grape variety, the vines must also be planted on the proper rootstocks. The wrong combination can create too much or too little leaf growth or make the vines susceptible to diseases, resulting in very unhappy and unhealthy vines and grapes of unacceptable quality. Phylloxera is not the only disease that requires the replanting of the entire vineyard to repel the scourge. There are many bugs, animals, and fungi that can prey upon the vine, especially the young and vulnerable.

After analyzing all of this information, the vines can finally go into the ground. It generally takes four years for a newly planted vineyard to reach productivity. If a vintner makes a wrong decision—plants the wrong grape for the soil or whatever, it may take seven or eight years before the error becomes apparent. Then the winemaker has lost the first hand in this high-stakes gamble. The ante has been raised and the game starts over.

Growing Season and Harvest

Vines must be nurtured during the growing season and the nature of the nurture varies with each vineyard. If the vines are prone to excessive vegetative growth, they must be pruned so the plant can concentrate on ripening the grapes.

Depending on the climate and degree of sunlight, leaf-pulling may be necessary to expose the grapes to the sun. In some cases, leaves are pulled on one side of the row to allow morning sunshine, but left in place on the other side to provide shade from the afternoon sun.

To limit a vine's yield to a desired level, the vintner may decide to prune bunches of fruit. Sometimes this pruning is done early in the season, shortly after the bunches form. Vintners often do a "green harvest," at the point of veraison—the time when grapes begin to soften and change color. At this moment, they can easily identify bunches that lag behind the majority in the ripening process. Pruning these less-ripe clusters ensures a more evenly ripe crop at harvest time.

Picking decisions are made on many criteria. Sugar levels in the grape juice—measured in degrees Brix or Beaumé or Oechsle, and so forth—are one factor. Some vintners look to other indicators of ripeness such as browning of the seeds or softening of the grape berries. Others use the ancient method of simply tasting the grapes. When the grapes achieve the perfect balance of sweet sugars and tart acids, it's time to pick.

As harvest approaches, presuming all has gone correctly thus far, the vintner must then worry about the weather. Even if the grapes are in perfect condition, every winemaker feels great apprehension as harvest time approaches. Will the good weather hold? Is there rain on the way that will swell the grapes, dilute the resultant wine, and cause rot? Is it too cold for the grapes to continue ripening? Is it too hot, causing the grapes to ripen too quickly, resulting in over-ripe, alcoholic wines? Will the picking crews be available when needed?

All these questions and more must be considered as the harvest time nears. Obviously, many of the answers cannot be known until the decision is made to pick.

In the Winery

A winemaker's job is that of a caretaker, interfering only when necessary during the transformation of grape juice to wine. The fewer intrusions made during the process, the easier the job becomes.

Suppose, then, that the grapes arrive at the winery in perfect shape. Now a whole new raft of decisions faces the quality-conscious producer.

All the incoming grapes must be inspected, and unripe bunches or unevenly ripe bunches set aside. Then the grapes are usually sent to a crusher/destemmer where the stems are removed and the skins of the grapes are broken.

One common innovation in modern winemaking is to allow the juice for both red and white wines to macerate with the grape skins for a few days prior to the start of fermentation. This cold maceration, or cold soaking, can enhance the richness, texture, bouquet, and color of the wine. Temperature control is absolutely necessary to accomplish this technique since fermenting yeasts remain dormant at low temperatures.

At this point, it is most common for the juice to be pumped to a fermenting vat. White wines normally are separated from their skins at this point. Red wines, though, are kept with the grape skins. The juice of most red grapes is white and the extraction of color for red wines comes from the skins of the grapes over a period of generally 7 to 21 days. Rosé wines stay with the grape skins for just a few hours to extract the lovely pink hue the winemaker desires.

The fermenting vessel is most often a stainless steel tank, but can be a barrel (large or small, new or used, any variety of wood), concrete vat, plastic tub, or other containment receptacle. Some vintners let the native or "wild" yeasts on the grape skins become the fermenting agents, but most commercial wines are injected with strains of yeast that do the most consistent job of fermenting the juice. The fermentation of grape juice into wine is a very complex process, with a cascade of some 50 or so chemical reactions required to create wine. Basically, though, the yeast consumes the sugar in the grape juice and converts it into alcohol and carbon dioxide gas.

A term that many serious wine drinkers have heard is malolactic fermentation. This is a biochemical process of converting malic acid into lactic acid and carbon dioxide. Lactic acid is a much "softer" acid thus giving a very smoothing taste and texture to the wine. All red wines undergo malo, but the choice must be made for whites, rosés; and sparklings. The correct bacteria and proper temperature are the necessary ingredients for malo to occur.

After fermentation is complete, the next decision to be made is aging. Is this a drink-it-now or slow-to-emerge type of wine? Does it need the taming effects of time in barrel, or just a short nap in the bottle? Barrels cost big bucks and require lots of maintenance. The winery owner must choose between a short-term and long-term capital investment when considering barrel aging.

Barrels, or barriques (French sounds fancier), can be made of any type of wood—oak, chestnut, redwood, beech, and pine have all been used at some point in history. Oak has proven to be the best material, whether it is from France, Yugoslavia, or America. Different oak varieties impart specific flavors. Different treatment of the oak also affects results. How long and where was the oak dried? How was it cut? Was it sawn or split? How was it toasted or charred? Was the entire barrel toasted or just the heads? Was it a light, medium, or heavy toast? If you ask winemakers, you will find strong proponents for particular forests, coopers, and toasting levels for each type of wine they make, and none of them agree!

Oak aging regimens vary greatly. Some winemakers use entirely new oak barrels. More often, economics dictate that barrels be used several times before they are relegated to lumber yard planter status. Thus, it is common for wines to age in second- or third-year barrels. With each use, the impact of the wood lessens and wines aged in older oak reveal much subtler nuances of the vanilla and baking spice components found in wines aged in new oak.

Winemakers must also decide how long to age in barrel, if that is their choice. Will it be six months in new wood plus one year in older barrels or vice-versa? Half in barrel and half in tank? Large barrels or small barrels? The biggest reds tend to spend more time in oak (up to two to three years and beyond), but the choice varies with the vintner. The possibilities are virtually endless.

Every barrel of wine is slightly different, however, and vintners must also decide whether to blend all barrels together and make one wine, or select the best barrels for a special reserve designation. The trade-off is obvious. If you take the best barrels out of the blend, you will be left with a lesser wine for the (now) secondary bottling.

After the aging and barrel blending decisions are made, there comes a time when the wine must be bottled and sent to market. Before bottling, vintners spend a great deal of time making trial blends of the various component wines to fine tune the final rendition to the desired style. When that decision is made, the wine is generally assembled in a large blending tank and sent to the bottling line.

At that point, the wine is bottled, labeled, and prepared for shipment. Many vintners choose to let the wine rest for a few weeks or months in bottle prior to release. The whole process can take from a few months for unoaked whites, rosés, and reds—to five years and more for the grandest of reserve wines.

On Your Palate

With such a multitude of choices to make during the transformation of grapes into wine, it's easy to see why there are so many different characteristics and nuances to wine. The world would be a very boring place if every wine were made the same way, from the same grape variety, employing the same methods. The joy of wine is in its differences and endless nuances of aroma and flavor.

Let us raise our glasses and celebrate that we get to choose from such an amazing array of fine wines. Diversity is king. Let it reign!!

Now that you have taken the dive into wine, you will find that there is so much more to explore. It is impossible to know everything about wine or to try every wine, but every new wine you taste adds to your sensory library.

If you have tasted all 60 grape varieties listed in this book, you are probably already interested in the next 60. After all, there are thousands of wine grape varieties to discover. Even if you have tasted wines from just five or ten new grapes, you have enhanced your tasting experience and better defined your personal preferences. You can add to your repertoire at a casual pace by making a point to try something new whenever you shop for a bottle or peruse a restaurant wine list.

If you had fun during your exploration, you can continue the enjoyment and start over again. Simply choose different examples of the grape varieties and you will doubly enhance your knowledge and experience.

If your interest and enthusiasm has
been piqued, join our online community at

www.divingintowine.com

Here you can compare notes with other similarly
enthusiastic "divers" and use each other's experiences
to enhance your exploration. You will also find
additional resources to expand and
enhance your wine discovery.